This coloring book belongs to :

____

a large brown animal with long thin legs. The adult male deer is called a stag and may have antlers growing from its head. The female deer is called a doe and a young deer is called a fawn

Letter D

dolphin

a large brown animal with long thin legs. The adult male deer is called a stag and may have antlers grow- ing from its head. The female deer is called a doe and a young deer is called a fawn

Letter D
Deer

A crocodile is a large reptile with a long body and strong jaws. Crocodiles live in rivers and eat meat.

letter c
crocodile

An owl is a bird with a flat face, large eyes, and a small sharp beak. Most owls obtain their food by hunting small animals at night and make a sound called hooting.

letter O
Owl

A peacock is a large bird. The male has a very large tail covered with blue and green spots, which it can spread out like a fan

letter P
peacock

a large African mammal with a very
long neck and forelegs, having a
coat patterned with brown patches
separated by lighter lines. It is the
tallest living animal.

letter G
Giraffe

a small to medium-sized primate
that typically has a long tail, most
kinds of which live in trees in trop-
ical countries.

letter M
monkey

A frog is a small animal with
smooth skin, big eyes, and long
back legs which it uses for jumping.
Frogs usually live near water

Letter F
Frog

a large black-and-white mammal,
similar to a bear, that lives in for-
ests in China and Tibet and eats
bamboo (stems of a type of grass).

letter P
Panda bear

a small animal covered in fur with a long tail. Squirrels climb trees and feed on nuts and seeds

Squirrel

a flightless swift-running African bird with a long neck, long legs, and two toes on each foot. It is the largest living bird, with males reaching a height of up to 2.75 m.

letter O
Ostrich

a small domesticated carnivorous mammal with soft fur, a short snout, and retractable claws. It is widely kept as a pet or for catching mice, and many breeds have been developed.

letter C
Cat

a fully grown female animal of a
domesticated breed of ox, kept to
produce milk or beef.

letter C
Cow

A lion is a large wild member of the cat family that is found in Africa and north-western India. Lions have yellowish fur, and male lions have long hair on their head and neck

Letter L
Lion

A cock is an adult male chicken.
The cock was announcing the start
of a new day.

Letter C
Cock

a warm-blooded egg-laying verte-
brate animal distinguished by the
possession of feathers, wings, a
beak, and typically by being able to
fly.

Letter B

bird

a wild carnivorous mammal which is the largest member of the dog family, living and hunting in packs. It is native to both Eurasia and North America, but is much perse-cuted and has been widely exter-minated.

Letter W
Wolf

a mythical animal typically rep-
resented as a horse with a single
straight horn projecting from its
forehead.

Letter U
Unicorn

a small animal that usually lives
in holes in the ground and has long
ears, soft fur, and back legs that
are longer than its front legs.

Letter R

Rabbit

An elephant is an enormous, four-footed animal with big ears and a long trunk. ... Elephants are the largest animals that live on land. They are spectacular animals, with curved ivory tusks on either side of a trunk that they use for grasping objects, vocalizing, and sucking up water to drink.

Letter E
Elephant

An octopus is a soft sea creature with eight long arms called tentacles which it uses to catch food. and living mostly at the bottom of the sea

Letter O
Octopus

a very large marine mammal with
a streamlined hairless body, a hori-
zontal tail fin, and a blowhole on
top of the head for breathing

Letter W
Whale

a long limbless reptile which has no eyelids, a short tail, and jaws that are capable of considerable extension. Some snakes have a venomous bite.

Letter S
Snake

a slow-moving typically herbivorous
land reptile of warm climates, en-
closed in a scaly or leathery domed
shell into which it can retract its
head and thick legs.

Letter T

Tortoise

an African wild horse with black-
and-white stripes and an erect
mane.

letter Z
Zebra